Hugs
and
love
to you
on your next
organizing
project!

MCPatti Langston

Decluttering Your Space and Your Mind

McPatti Langston

MOUNTAIN ARBOR
    PRESS
Alpharetta, GA

Although the author and publisher have made every effort to ensure that the information in this book was correct at the time of first publication, the author and publisher do not assume and hereby disclaim any liability to any party for any loss, damage, or disruption caused by errors or omissions, whether such errors or omissions result from negligence, accident, or any other cause.

Copyright © 2018 by Patricia Langston

All rights reserved. No part of this book may be reproduced or transmitted in any form or by any means, electronic or mechanical, including photocopying, recording, or any information storage and retrieval system, without permission in writing from the author.

ISBN: 978-1-63183-356-4 - Paperback
ISBN: 978-1-63183-379-3 - ePub
ISBN: 978-1-63183-380-9 - Mobi

Library of Congress Control Number: 2018962086

Printed in the United States of America   1 1 0 6 1 8

⊗This paper meets the requirements of ANSI/NISO Z39.48-1992 (Permanence of Paper)

Cover art by Preston Lindsay
Back cover photo by Marchet Butler

To my mom, for teaching me the value of organization.

Contents

Acknowledgments ix

Part I: The Queen's Journey — Learning to Let Go
    Introduction to Part I 3
    Chapter 1: The Queen's Clutter 5
    Chapter 2: The Five Dragons of Contention — The Dragon of Resistance 9
    Chapter 3: The Dragon of Attachment 15
    Chapter 4: The Dragon of Distraction 19
    Chapter 5: The Dragon of Frustration 23
    Chapter 6: The Dragon of Fear 29
    Chapter 7: Downsizing — Letting Go to Grow 33

Part II: Creating Your Own Organizing Story for Your New Life
    Introduction to Part II 39
    Chapter 8: It's a Closet Affair 41
    Chapter 9: Kitchen Catch-all 47
    Chapter 10: Clearing the Carriage 53
    Chapter 11: Freedom in Your Workplace 57
    Chapter 12: The Nuts and Bolts of Organizing 65
    Chapter 13: Organizing with Children 71

Conclusion 75

Acknowledgments

I would like to express my sincere gratitude to everyone who supported me on the journey of writing this book. The encouragement has been amazing, and I want to thank you all for motivating me to even begin the writing process, much less make it to the finish line!

I want to thank my husband, Bruce, and my son, Dillon, for their continued support. Super kudos to Preston Lindsay, my amazing graphic artist and illustrator of the cover of this book, for inspiring me every step of the way. I really can't thank him enough for the motivation and inspiration on this project. Jemille Williams, a super talented writer herself, inspired me to be the organizer I am today. She believed in my talents and trusted me as an organizer and designer, and her support helped launch me into this career path. Thanks to Cathryn Marshall for her suggestion that I write a book about organization, her positive words of encouragement, and believing that I could inspire others to organize. Beth Teague, for helping me focus on not losing sight of where I was going with this book. To Clarisse for attending the incessant shenanigans. To Joyce Rennolds, my mentor and spiritual advisor, who told me that I have a book inside me. Her light and encouragement helped me to get this far. Also to Miss Meowster, my cat, for being totally *purrfect* and cute.

Finally, big hugs and squeezes to all my clients who have organizational challenges that I have been on this journey with, learning about what you needed and how the process changed your life, your mind, and your spirit. Thanks for the lessons.

Part I

The Queen's Journey—
Learning to Let Go

Introduction to Part I

I've worked with many different clients over the years. I like to think of them as my queens and kings, and I am but their humble sorceress. As their organizational sorceress, I guide them to a new way to enjoy their castles. We get the muck out of their moats. We declutter the king's court and dust off the drawbridge. After all, your home is your "castle," your "royal domain." Shouldn't you enjoy life in your own home?

The number-one obstacle to having a "crystal-clear castle" is clutter. The subject of clutter will be covered extensively as you read this book.

Through my experience, clients face a series of "dragons" in their quests to declutter their castles—dragons that threaten their castles and prevent them from dealing with the paralyzing clutter around them. The biggest dragon, if you will, is called resistance. It is inevitable that feelings of resistance will pop up, sometimes quite strongly. The feeling of resistance can make you feel confused and want to run the other way. You may feel that this dragon is holding you hostage. Don't despair! The fire-breathing Dragon of Resistance can be tricky and immobilizing; however, when dealt with gently and consistently, we can put that scary dragon in its place.

Dragons, as we call them, can be dealt with, and you can learn to take your life back from clutter. Accept any feelings you might have about this process, and most importantly, *continue at your own pace*! If you push yourself too hard, you will quit. Remember, if there weren't any resistance, your castle would already be cleared and organized!

Getting started seems to be the most challenging part of organization because of the fear of criticism, doubt, and negativity. You need to breathe. Let go of all those evil thoughts, and move forward to the first step of your new organizing journey. To getting started on your new journey, I say congratulations! Let's begin.

Chapter 1

The Queen's Clutter

Once upon a time, Queen Hodgepodge and King Haywire lived in a very cluttered castle. There were tchotchkes in the kitchen, piles in the parlor, buildups in the bathrooms! There was so much stuff in every nook and cranny that the queen had no idea where to begin organizing; just the thought of getting started triggered anxiety.

Being the queen, she didn't want to ask for help. That showed weakness . . . right? And the queen *never* showed weakness. It just wasn't royal!

Finally, she admitted her discomfort at seeing all the disarray everywhere. She found it too embarrassing to invite people over to the castle with it looking such a fright. Unfortunately, with cutbacks in the castle's budget, she had to let her housekeeping staff go. It was now all up to her. She felt oh-so incapable of bearing this burden all by her lonesome! If only she could find a way to manage the castle clutter on her own . . .

***

Like Queen Hodgepodge, you, too, may feel self-conscious when someone else is present while you're decluttering and sorting through belongings. After all, your castle is a reflection of yourself, and if it's a disorderly mess, you may feel apprehensive about how people may judge you if they see it. That is okay. However, constantly having to look for things wastes time and increases your anxiety levels. Try not to be too hard on yourself.

Clutter is just an overaccumulation of things out of their proper places. For example, when your china cabinet is full of action figures instead of your mother's prized dinner plates. Clutter is anything that fills your space in a disorganized way, leaving you stressed out and unable to function efficiently. It can come in many forms, such as stacks of old bills, school papers to sign, unread magazines, a basket full of mending, unfolded laundry, unfinished craft projects, or an overstocked kitchen.

Domestic disorganization can make your brain feel as scattered as your home. However, it can all be dealt with and eliminated when you streamline your castle into zones that can be easily dealt with.

There are several advantages to removing clutter, like feeling calmer, more centered, and in control. All of the people who have decluttered their spaces with me have expressed that it helped create more clarity in all aspects of their lives. The truth is, when you get rid of the stuff you don't need and don't really love, you're left with just the good stuff, which builds you up instead of dragging you down. The most important thing is that you feel good about yourself.

Envision being free of clutter and no longer drowning in debris; no more being showered in old cereal because the box keeps falling from the overstuffed cabinets. You can get rid of cumbersome clutter if you are willing. The hardest part of beginning this process is making the choice to get rid of things.

You must be willing to let things leave your home that no longer serve you or reflect your current self. Release it and let it go. If it reminds you of a person or experience that has left your life, then let that item go, too. The best way to ultimately honor yourself and create a home that reflects your best self is to only allow things that have a place in your current life to stay.

A good starting place is to establish some realistic boundaries for yourself. We often think of boundaries as something external, like a kingdom keeping ogres at bay or a fence around your yard to keep wild boars out. However, we're talking about boundaries in regard to the process of decluttering. We are talking about *personal* boundaries: what we let in and allow to accumulate, and what we throw out. One could say that the process of organizing and decluttering *is* the process of developing strong personal boundaries.

Since decluttering and organizing is a process (and no one ever does it perfectly from the start), you need to keep practicing these new habits so that you are making progress. The more you practice, the easier it becomes! You could say that this process is really a spiritual commitment to manifesting calm contentment.

It is my hope that after reading this book, you will have learned functioning systems designed to address your personal boundaries for how much clutter you are willing to tolerate in your space and in your life, and that they will serve you in keeping your castle clean, clear, and clutter-free.

TIPS FOR MANAGING CLUTTER IN YOUR LIFE

Go through the belongings you're trying to organize and put them into three separate boxes or piles:

- Keep
- Give away
- Throw away

A good way to address that third "throw away" pile is to ask yourself these three questions:

- *Do I use it?*
- *Do I enjoy it?*
- *Can I replace it if I should ever need it?*

Answering these questions about individual items will help you to assess their usefulness in your life. If you'll never use it, don't enjoy it, or can replace it, then you're in a good place to let that item go!

Once you have a pile of keepers, categorize them and keep multiples of one item together, i.e. candles, blankets, arts and crafts, first-aid items, etc. Enjoy the gentle calm of orderly items!

AFFIRMATIONS AND EXERCISES FOR GROWTH

MIND: Assess which room needs to be dealt with immediately for functionality. The best rooms to start with are usually the rooms that are most often used. For example, the kitchen, bathroom, or office.

BODY: Designate sections of the room for where your supplies, workspace (maybe a table for packing and organizing), and things to donate, give away, recycle, and trash will be.

SPIRIT: Keep repeating to yourself that this process is going easily and effortlessly, with peace and harmony. You will feel lighter and freer as you release these items that no longer serve you.

CHAPTER 1 ACTION PLAN

- Visualize your home the way you'd like it to be (30-second meditation).
- Which area (zone) of your space needs immediate attention? _____
- List five things you can get rid of this week:
    1. _____
    2. _____
    3. _____
    4. _____
    5. _____

Chapter 2

The Five Dragons of Contention—The Dragon of Resistance

Queen Hodgepodge felt paralyzed with fear. Did she see what she thought she saw? She looked out the window tentatively, and YES! She could see the dragon's blue scales as the beast slithered through the trees toward the castle. What could she do? She was no match for the dragon, and it was unlikely anyone else would admit they even saw it. One rule of dragons is that you never admit that they are there. Just pretend everything's fine, and they will eventually go away . . . right?

Long ago, when the queen was only a princess, anytime she felt afraid or apprehensive, her mind would manifest her fear into visions of looming and formidable dragons. Even as an adult, they would slither back into her life any time she felt nervous, worried, or stressed.

The closer the blue dragon got to the castle, the more anxious the queen felt. She was having a hard time even breathing now. The queen's misgivings about parting with her sentimental pieces was the reason the dragon drew ever nearer. How could she get rid of any of her precious *things*? What if she threw something out that she might need later?

The king could see her resistance to the idea of letting things go, but he really didn't understand. After all, stuff is just stuff! So, in a high and mighty tone, King Haywire told his queen to just deal with it and get the castle organized.

How could he be so cold? These things held precious memories for the queen, and she wasn't going to get rid of just anything and everything! For instance, the baby bottle the prince had once used was now cracked, but it was still his baby bottle. And that cute little dress that the princess had worn for her kindergarten graduation. She had looked so sweet! How could Queen Hodgepodge let this *stuff*—these *memories*—go?

***

Any kingdom complete with a castle and royal family must surely have a dragon or two lurking around. Like many of us, Queen Hodgepodge was battling several metaphorical dragons, specifically the five Dragons of Contention: resistance, attachment, distraction, frustration, and fear.

These dastardly dragons are often the culprits behind people's aversion to organizing and decluttering their lives. Each of these dragons ultimately stems from anxiety, and can therefore be very daunting to face. So, take a deep breath and affirm that you can do this and that you will find harmony through this process. Now, grab your sharpest sword and let's tackle those nasty beasts together!

The biggest and gnarliest dragon for people to face is the Dragon of Resistance. With fearsome eyes and yellow talons, it pins you to the ground, inhibiting you from moving or addressing the disarray. Its sheer size seems to block everything else from view.

During the process of decluttering and organizing, it is inevitable that feelings, perhaps even very strong ones, will come up. These feelings may immobilize and confuse you. Do not despair! Accept any feelings you may have about the process.

It is normal to feel resistance in letting go of things that you have held on to for years. After all, you would not have kept them if there weren't some kind of resistance to letting them go in the first place. Some things may have stories attached to them. For example, you may have kept a special corsage from your first date with your Prince Charming . . . which is actually the time that the two of you got rip-roaring drunk in the back of a "borrowed" carriage and he puked on your new glass slippers. A fond memory nevertheless!

Likewise, you might have things of sentimental value that have been handed down from ruler to ruler over many years. Other things have monetary value, which you will need to determine before making a decision to keep or toss. Then there are things you may think you will need in the future. And there will always be items that you're not sure why you've even been hanging on to.

Let's say you have a favorite tiara—the one you got in Bavaria on your honeymoon. Its emerald-green gems are very worn, and some of the stones have fallen out. You never wear it, but it is still taking up space in your jewelry box. Every time you get dressed, this tiara gets in your way, so why do you still have it committed to your collection? Maybe you could write a story about it, document why it was important to you, or take a photo of it so you will always remember how it looked. Why not give it to another princess in the kingdom so it can be repaired and enjoyed by someone else? There are so many reasons to hang onto this tiara, but you need to change your thinking into ways you could feel good about letting it go.

Here are some things to consider that might make you less resistant to the idea of parting with your things:

- *Could someone else appreciate this?*
- *Will this item ever be of use to me again?*
- *Do I want to spend the time and money required to fix it?*

- *Would throwing it away have a serious impact on my life?*
- *How much would I really miss it?*
- *Would some organization be grateful to have this item?*
- *Do I have more than one?*
- *Is the item outdated, or has it outlived its usefulness?*
- *And most importantly, is this item adding to my life or taking away from it?*

It is important to know your strengths as well as your limitations. Remember to take things one step at a time and not overdo it. The general recommendation is to not go longer than three to four hours per organizing session. If you need to, break up larger tasks into smaller increments, even if the first task is just making a list of the areas that you feel you can best tackle. Divide large tasks into as many smaller steps as you need in order to get into action.

Another suggestion is to invite a friend over who will support you through the process. If you need an extra push, hire an organizer, preferably someone who has experience with resistance and attachment to household things.

A lot of people struggle with the Dragon of Resistance, and may have been avoiding the room(s) that need the most clearing for many years! They may feel that they lack the skills to declutter and organize their castle. There are also people who are overweight and fear that they are not physically up to the task. One person even confessed to me that she felt like "a tortoise in a world of hares." There are even those who are so resistant that they will not allow anyone to help them! Some queens and kings even secretly pull worthless items out of the trash after a day's work, undoing much of the good work that's been done.

If you want to defeat the Dragon of Resistance and extinguish its flames, then pick up your sword and cut the strings of control! Finding a way to relinquish your need to be in control will help you let go of the things you've maintained a hold on. As you give in to the energy of letting go, you will find that your new organizational systems give you the control over your domain that you truly need!

AFFIRMATIONS AND EXERCISES FOR GROWTH

MIND: Try to relax. Take a few minutes for deep breathing while you clear your mind.

BODY: Put on some soothing music, or anything that relaxes and/or energizes you to get into the organizing mood.

SPIRIT: Light some candles. Pretend you are performing a sacred ritual. After all, physical decluttering can lead to mental decluttering, as well.

CHAPTER 2 ACTION PLAN

- Take three long, slow, deep breaths, reaffirming to yourself that you can do this.
- What aspects of your life have gotten you to this point, causing resistance in beginning this process?
  _____
- List three positive thoughts about parting with your things:
  1. _____
  2. _____
  3. _____

Chapter 3

The Dragon of Attachment

Queen Hodgepodge stood looking out the castle window toward the forest. *When will it come? When will the Dragon of Attachment come for me?* In her mind, this dragon was almost as big as the other, blue dragon, and she just couldn't see any way to defeat it. This dragon was all white. On the surface, this dragon was very pretty to look at. It had horns—lots of horns—like a crown of its own. It also had deep, black eyes and talons that seemed to disappear into the dragon's toes, only to be snapped out at a moment's notice. The wings were almost lace-like, and they flowed like a bride's dress train.

The queen saw it flying toward the castle just as she began going through the items from her kids' childhoods. It seemed like every item was too precious to let go, too precious to give away to someone who might make use of it. It was like trying to give away her own arm.

The queen looked lovingly at all her treasures, like the blanket she once wrapped her sweet little son in, the rattle her daughter used to laugh at when it made its sound, the hats they had worn during various Easter egg hunts. How in the world could she possibly let these things go? Weren't they far too valuable? In fact, weren't they irreplaceable?

Lost in thought, Queen Hodgepodge didn't see the Dragon of Attachment as it slithered into the castle. Its white scales made it almost translucent, and it seemed to disappear wherever it stopped.

***

You pick it up and caress it, think about it, and smile as you dust it off, but you cannot come up with a single reason as to why you are still hanging on to it. Why? It's that ghastly Dragon of Attachment! The "it" could be anything—a souvenir, an heirloom, gifts from a court jester whom you have not seen in years—anything! You must ask yourself these questions: Have you used it in the last year? Does it enhance your castle aesthetic? Does it reflect who you are in your life right now? If the answer is "no," what in gnome's name are you hanging onto it for?

The answer is attachment.

Of the five Dragons of Contention, attachment is right up there with resistance. It is arguably the biggest obstacle to decluttering. Attachment is an energy that has no logic, but it is strong and can be overpowering to the point of detriment. Attachment is a manifestation of anxiety. People develop attachments to their things in order to maintain control and to create the illusion of safety. This can make parting with them a very emotional and challenging process, and is often the reason that people maintain their cluttered ways. They feel as though they need their possessions so that they can be happy or functional when, in reality, it is that collection of unnecessary artifacts that is a main cause of the dysfunction in their space.

There are times that you see an item, whatever it is, and you can't use it, but you love it. You don't want to display it, you can't fix it or sell it, you don't even need it, but you still have it and you don't want to let it go. Discovering your reasons for holding on to any particular item can help you realize why you're developing certain attachments in the first place. While it is challenging, it can be fought head on.

Wade the Worrisome Wizard, for example, has dueled with this dragon before. Wade had a very large, vintage spellcasting book and would not part with it. Mind you, he had not looked at the book in years, and it was only taking up space and collecting dust on his bookshelf. He no longer needed this book, though it was well made and had once been very useful, as he had memorized all the major spells. However, the book was given to him by his favorite uncle, now deceased, and Wade just could not detach from it.

His organizing sorceress suggested he sell the book and use the money for something he really enjoys. Still, Wade could not let it go. It was a beautiful book, so she suggested he donate it to the local apothecary for young wizards and witches in training. Still, he could not part with it.

Suddenly, an idea! Wade was asked if he knew anyone personally who could benefit from a book of spells. He replied yes, he knew of someone who might: a young girl in his own village who just got her very first magic wand. How would he feel about giving this book to her as a gift?

He stopped and quietly thought about it. While he contemplated, the McOrganizing Sorceress reminded him, "At least you will always know where your book is—in the hands of someone you care about and who will take care of it. Don't think of it as letting the book go, but as transferring it to its proper home." He agreed, and upon offering the book to the girl, he saw how delighted she was as she thumbed through its pages. He left the girl's house feeling elated, knowing he gave her something that could bring her so much joy. In doing this one, seemingly simple act, his illogical attachment was totally dissolved, and the Dragon of Attachment slain.

With this life lesson learned, Wade can now remember this

strategy the next time the dragon rears its ugly head. He has continued to use this method of fending off attachment many times since then.

AFFIRMATIONS AND EXERCISES FOR GROWTH

MIND: You can enjoy peace of mind by releasing items to a charity, friend, or relative.

BODY: Your physical space is now being cleared, and clearing helps you release more items.

SPIRIT: Remember that when we let go of things that no longer serve our higher good, we make room for new and better things, adding to our spiritual wellbeing.

CHAPTER 3 ACTION PLAN

- Pick a special item in your castle and let it go to someone you know will enjoy it.
- When you released the item, how did you feel? Anxious? Happy? Relieved?

_____
_____
_____

- How can you keep the memories from an experience with a specific sentimental item while letting the physical item go?

_____
_____
_____

CHAPTER 4

THE DRAGON OF DISTRACTION

Oh! Look at all the pretty colors! Queen Hodgepodge thought. *It looks like a carnival!*

The Dragon of Distraction got her, hook, line, and sinker! As it moved, its multicolored scales flashed and sparkled. It possessed no real fangs like the Dragons of Resistance or Attachment; it didn't need them. This dragon found it so easy to distract humans from the important stuff and keep them very busy doing nothing, it was almost boring!

The queen was so interested in watching the small dragon dance around that she completely forgot what she was doing. Just then, King Haywire walked in. "I thought you were going to get this stuff cleaned up and organized," the king stated.

"I am," she stammered. "I just got a bit distracted by this colorful little dragon."

The dragon was nowhere in sight.

"Dragon? Where is there a dragon? I'll kill every last one of them . . ." The king got very serious as he bellowed, "BUT THEY DON'T EXIST! Now, get back to cleaning this mess up or I'll take care of it for you!" The king walked off in a huff, his face as red as Queen Hodgepodge had ever seen it.

That was all the incentive the queen needed to get back to her organizing.

***

Flashing its bright, shiny scales is the ostentatious Dragon of Distraction. Having too many distractions is one of the main reasons people in our society feel resistance toward completing organizing projects. With so many choices and temptations out there, many suffer from a fear of missing out, or "FOMO." They can't even plan a laundry night because they fear "missing out" on something better going on "out there!"

The truth is, if you plan well and execute that plan, you can have a lot of extra time for whatever is going on "out there." An added bonus is the relaxing peace you'll feel from a job well done.

When you are distracted by all the fluff out there, you are more likely to avoid completing certain tasks. Facebook, Twitter, Snapchat, and other social-media outlets can certainly bring joy and productivity (when used correctly) to your life, but when not used correctly, they can be vampires—leeches that suck time and productivity away from you. If you absolutely must use them, set a short time limit and stick to it. When the time is done, set the social media aside and move on to what you have planned for yourself in the way of task completion.

Beyond being easily distracted—or perhaps because of it—Queen Hodgepodge also struggled with time management. Having good time-management skills leaves you less stressed because you have a plan of action for how your time is being spent. You are more productive, as you have more energy and time to accomplish things.

What do you do with your time? What are your priorities? How do you schedule your appointments? Do you put your to-do items in your calendar? What are you doing to complete your tasks? Perhaps you delegate responsibilities to other people, or resort to lowering your standards and expectations. What are your biggest time wasters? Get real! They are often social media, phone calls, eating, watching TV, etc. You can cut back on the time wasting by implementing some basic habits for yourself. Try setting a specific time in your schedule for email responses and returning phone calls. If you have a busy family, it might be helpful to keep a master calendar for each family member's activities in a central area where you keep appointment reminders, invites, and events recorded.

Take thirty minutes every morning to plan your day. The earlier in the day you plan, the better the outcome in terms of productivity and lowering stress. Defining daily, weekly, and monthly goals is helpful in planning your schedule so that these goals can be met. However, it's also important not to be too structured. If you overschedule everything down to the second, and something goes amiss, your whole schedule is ruined. Be sure to leave room for error and spontaneity!

AFFIRMATIONS AND EXERCISES FOR GROWTH

MIND: Make weekly appointments (same date and time every week) for individual, regularly occurring tasks.

- Scheduling them at the same time each week makes the tasks easier to remember.
- Treat the appointments the same as you would any major appointment.
- Do your best to not break or reschedule them.

BODY: Be still in preparation for the decluttering process.

- Tell yourself, "I can complete this work today."

- Don't beat yourself up if you didn't get it all done last week. Just keep moving forward.

SPIRIT: Stay in the present moment. Do not focus on the future or past while organizing.

- Dwelling on the past is like trying to put toothpaste back in the tube.
- You can't change the past. Learn from it and move forward.
- Live in the present and use it to make positive changes for your future.

CHAPTER 4 ACTION PLAN

- List five things that distract you from your organizing goals:
    1. _____
    2. _____
    3. _____
    4. _____
    5. _____

- Set a boundary to limit each of your distractions:
    1. _____
    2. _____
    3. _____
    4. _____
    5. _____

- Pick a night, realistically, that can be your "organizing night." This frees up your schedule on other nights, which helps in tackling FOMO.

CHAPTER 5

THE DRAGON OF FRUSTRATION

Queen Hodgepodge couldn't see the invisible Dragon of Frustration, but goodness, was she frustrated! It had been many years since the last time the queen had to prepare for such a big move. In addition to the decluttering of her daily accumulations, there was furniture to be moved, clothes to be sorted through, and oh, the paper clutter left to file! As she mulled over all of this in her mind, she moved her fashion magazines to where the books were, and moved the books to where the magazines had been. She was doing lots of work, but not really getting anything done. No matter what she tried, it seemed as if nothing got cleaned or organized.

Feeling so overwhelmed that she just couldn't stand it anymore, the queen cried, "I need help!"

At that moment, the royal messenger entered the room. "Your Highness, there is someone at the gate asking to see you. She said that you called her and asked her to come," the messenger stated.

"Well . . . who is she? I don't recall asking anyone for—" Queen Hodgepodge stopped midsentence, remembering her cry for help. "Have a guard show her in. And . . . tell him to stay with us until I relieve him."

"Yes, Your Highness!"

When the McOrganizing Sorceress entered the room, she looked up at the queen and said, "You called for some help. I came as fast as I could. You are battling dragons, I presume?"

"Well, yes. There have been several dragons around here lately, but I don't see any here now."

"Are you frustrated because you don't seem to be getting anywhere?"

"Yes, yes I am!" Queen Hodgepodge declared. "I am working my fingers to the bone trying to get organized, and I am not making any apparent progress."

The McOrganizing Sorceress replied, "Do you have any systems or processes in place to ward off those dragons? Without systems and processes, it is easy for the dragons to keep you from really doing anything, even though you are seemingly doing a lot!" She continued, "Show me what we are up against here. I'll help you slay those dragons once and for all!"

Queen Hodgepodge could see the confidence in the McOrganizing Sorceress's eyes and just knew that she could trust her to help with all of this. Finally, she was beginning to feel hopeful!

***

Frustration is a temporary emotional state that, with some time and effort, always passes. Queen Hodgepodge felt exceedingly frustrated because she had unrealistic expectations for managing her castle. It was time to declutter over twenty years' worth of stuff, and although she was working hard and frequently, she felt angry, agitated, and annoyed because she was not seeing a lot of progress. She knew that part of the problem was that she had been throwing pity parties for herself and was in a toxic, "poor me" state of mind. The queen wanted to be at the end of the decluttering project, even though her journey had only just begun!

She talked about these self-imposed barriers and limitations with the McOrganizing Sorceress. The McOrganizing Sorceress told her she could battle the dragons clouding her mind by learning how to deal with her anxiety, frustrations, and fears. She then taught the queen some meditations and relaxing breathing techniques. Breathing in for three counts, holding for three counts, and exhaling for three counts helped Queen Hodgepodge lower her anxiety levels and see more clearly that her expectations were too high.

The queen and her sorceress discussed the benefits of expressing frustration, including gaining clarity from lowering expectations and creating a more realistic timetable for progress. The McOrganizing Sorceress then promised to return to the castle a couple times a week to help motivate Queen Hodgepodge in her decluttering project.

One day during one of the McOrganizing Sorceress's visits, the queen concluded it was her own poor organization skills that had brought her to this overly cluttered state. She realized that if she were more organized, she would have more leisure time. Further, the more organized her stuff, the more organized her mind would feel, leaving plenty of energy to dedicate to kingdom trivialities. Simplifying her life was the answer; less stuff, less problems!

It's easier to maintain a small system, rather than a larger system, when organizing. So, instead of focusing on organizing the whole castle at once, Queen Hodgepodge and the McOrganizing Sorceress talked about focusing on only one closet at a time. They also decided to *not* move everything out of the castle—that was an old rule—instead deciding to take one small section, remove only those things that need to be eliminated, organize what's left, and then move onto the next section. Finally, focusing on what had been accomplished rather than what was still left to do helped the queen feel more at ease.

In the weeks that ensued, the McOrganizing Sorceress saw the queen thrive by lowering her expectations and releasing more castle clutter. Queen Hodgepodge's frustration level lowered as her passion for decluttering increased.

AFFIRMATIONS AND EXERCISES FOR GROWTH

MIND: Instead of focusing on your project as a whole, take it step by step.

- Breaking large tasks into smaller ones will make it easier to complete the large task.
- By completing one smaller section, you get a sense of accomplishment that will help you with each successive section.

BODY: When you are frustrated, a change of scenery can give you a new perspective. Take a walk to renew your spirit and lower your frustration levels.

- Doing a physical activity like walking gets endorphins flowing, which will help calm your frustrations.
- Going to a different room or a different part of your yard can also lighten your mental load and make things easier.

SPIRIT: Focus on positive affirmations that help you move forward in clarity.

- Try to think about good things or good times in your life.
- Think of strategies that might help with the task at hand.
- If you tell yourself you can or you can't, you are right. If that is the case, why not tell yourself that you can?

CHAPTER 5 ACTION PLAN

- Learn to recognize when you're frustrated by asking yourself the following questions. If you answer "yes" to more than one of these questions, frustration may be the reason.

    1. Have you been working on the same thing for more than a reasonable amount of time?
    2. Are you finding yourself getting angry during this process?
    3. Do you feel like you are spinning your wheels but going nowhere?
    4. Are you ready to give up?

- If you're frustrated, put down whatever you are working on and take a two-minute break. If you find that you still can't come back to that particular task, move forward with another task and address the challenging one at another time.
- Do not let frustration deter you from completing your journey! Try writing down your frustrations to help you work through them, or at least to acknowledge other possible underlying causes of your distress.

_____
_____
_____
_____
_____

Chapter 6

The Dragon of Fear

One day, the McOrganizing Sorceress came to meet with Queen Hodgepodge for an organizing session and found the queen nervous and anxious. It was obvious that the green-bellied Dragon of Fear had paid her a visit. After some prodding from the McOrganizing Sorceress, Queen Hodgepodge admitted her fear of being judged on how many things she owned. The closets were her sanctuary, her own private domain. She felt paralyzed by fear of potential judgment from others, which was really a reflection of her own self-doubt. Her worries stemmed from her fear of what other people thought of her. Would the McOrganizing Sorceress think she's a hoarder? What if she wasn't ready to release anything? Would the McOrganizing Sorceress criticize her for her choices? What's more, how long would organizing take? What financial cost would this service require?

Queen Hodgepodge feared opening her credit-card statements, knowing she'd have to face her sizeable shopping obsession. Her closets were stacked with dirty clothes, and she refused to let anyone—including the maids and the king—come into the closets, despite her loathing of doing the laundry.

In truth, the queen's biggest fear was that someone, anyone, would know her secret: that she had another side to her that the kingdom had not seen. She never wanted anyone to see that her inner mind was messy, disorganized, and that she struggled juggling her life and keeping it organized.

The Dragon of Fear had all these fearful thoughts running through the queen's head, adding to her resistance to begin the process. Facing the dragon head on, she told the McOrganizing Sorceress the truth: She was, in fact, a very messy queen, and she did NOT have any systems for maintaining her stuff. She needed a new vein of energy to help her clear this castle of clutter.

Had Queen Hodgepodge not confronted the Dragon of Fear about to devour her, it would have ruined her mental and physical health and stopped her from moving forward. The McOrganizing Sorceress, of course, understood that organizing was not the queen's forte, so they started working together to develop a system that could be used every day from then on to keep her life under control.

***

Now is the time to address any anxieties or poor time management that may be contributing to your fear. At this point the Dragons of Contention are in your head, trying to bring you down. Their negative and toxic chatter may exaggerate any feelings of inadequacy you may possess, and lead you to believe that you are unworthy or incapable of dealing with your life in a constructive, positive fashion.

Banish those negative emotions with your magic wand! We are on to the next step in our journey of cleanliness, and our goal is clarity.

Consider the benefits of decluttering and organizing. When you first start getting organized and changing your space, the immediate payoff is that you will begin to destress, lowering the hormones in your body that are related to stress, which will help elevate your mood. Living in an uncomfortable kingdom is a reflection of your mentality, so you may want to hire a professional organizer to help you change your energy. This will allow you to make the necessary changes to your space and help you feel better about yourself!

The more your space changes, the more you will change, and more will come into your life that is positive and affirming.

AFFIRMATIONS AND EXERCISES FOR GROWTH MIND:

- *I will face the fear of my dragons today and not give in.*
- *I will think positive thoughts today and not let the dragons steal my time.*

BODY:

- *Fear does not paralyze me anymore. I am able to move freely and effortlessly in my body.*
- *I will work on one task at a time and not take on more than what is immediately in front of me.*

SPIRIT:

- *I let go of fearful thoughts and negative memories. I am clear to move forward.*
- *I will think positive thoughts today and not let the dragons steal my joy.*

CHAPTER 6 ACTION PLAN

- When fear interjects itself into your thoughts, it is important to have a solid mantra to look to for encouragement. Repeat aloud to yourself: "I am not afraid to achieve my goals."

- Visualize your space as clear and open, and think about how empowered you will feel when everything is complete. Write about how you want to feel at the end of this process to help you envision your goal.

  _____
  _____

- Sometimes the fear can begin to consume you. When it gets to be too much, hire an organizer so you don't have to work through it on your own. Asking for help is always an option, so use it to your advantage!

Chapter 7

Downsizing—Letting Go to Grow

King Haywire told Queen Hodgepodge that, once he handed over the kingdom to their eldest daughter, he and his queen would be moving to the royal beach condo. The king was very much looking forward to living on the beach. Why, he had even purchased a surfboard!

After successfully purchasing the condo, next came the dreaded process of downsizing. Queen Hodgepodge knew this day would come, and she was feeling particularly anxious about downsizing. She stared down the daunting task of sorting through household belongings without any clue of where to start. The palace was full of furniture and accessories: her numerous collections of phoenix-feather boas, jewels gathered from the Great Glitz mines, her decorative toadstools, a sizeable collection of enormous clay pots, and so much more.

"What to do with all of this stuff?" she bemoaned.

Now all the dragons came roaring back in her head. How to start? What to keep? What not to keep? What to do with what they didn't keep? She felt overwhelmed, but then she took a deep breath and thought of all the advice the McOrganizing Sorceress had given her over the past few weeks.

She could do this!

***

When taking on a large downsizing project, you should start by setting up your workstation. Pick a room to begin in, and have all your pens, sticky notes, boxes, and tape in one place. Next, it is important to do some preplanning, as you want the process to be as organized and efficient as possible.

First, discuss your priorities for the move and address your needs for the new space. When moving from a larger home to a smaller one, it is often easiest to begin with decisions about furniture: How many beds will you need? Are there too many large pieces to fit in the new space? Determining right off the bat what you need to keep will make apparent the things that you now have no place for.

Second, take some time to envision yourself in your new space. How do you see yourself spending your time? This will aid in your ability to eliminate things that you will no longer have a use for, thus cutting down on the later decluttering process.

After preplanning, the time will come for you to remove the items you've deemed unnecessary to your new life. There are three distinct possibilities for what you can do with these items: Store them for future use, donate or sell them, or dispose of them.

With a project this large, it is suggested that you work through the house one room at a time. While working, make a pile of items to be thrown away and, if possible, place anything going to your new home in one location. Be realistic about what you will use in the next space. Try to eliminate larger items first. Remember, you are moving into a smaller home and will need as much space as you can get.

If you are not sure about the next space and what you will use, get a storage unit and take items you cannot decide on to the unit. After you get a better feel for what will fit in the new space, you can return to those items to make a final decision.

Although you want to deal with as many things before the move as possible, obtaining a storage unit is a good option if you're really struggling with multiple items and don't have the time to deliberate.

Similar to the helpful questions to ask yourself from Chapter 2, the following are questions to keep in mind while downsizing that will help you figure out what to do with your stuff:

- *Do I love the item?*
- *Is the item useful to me now?*
- *Will the item add value to my life?*
- *Do I have duplicates of this item?*
- *Can I replace this item if I needed to?*
- *On a scale of 1–10, how attached am I to this item?*
- *Could someone else find value in this item?*

AFFIRMATIONS AND EXERCISES FOR GROWTH MIND:

- Plan well, and stick to that plan. It will help you.
- Stay focused to do what is needed.

BODY:

- Pace yourself. Pick a time to work during the day when you have the most energy.
- Do a little bit at a time. Don't try to accomplish the whole thing in one session.

SPIRIT:

- Play some fun music or listen to an audiobook that eases the spirit while working.

- Acknowledge what is completed, not what you still have left to do.

CHAPTER 7 ACTION PLAN

- The biggest advantage you can give yourself is to preplan early, so you can make the most of your items. Draft a plan for your largest items to keep, store, or give away.

Item	Keep, Store, or Give Away

Part II

Creating Your Own Organizing Story for Your New Life

Introduction to Part II

The second half of this book follows Queen Hodgepodge as she learns how to face the dragons, develop effective tools, and start organizing her many collections. She is gaining skills and creating a new blueprint to clear her clutter to better ease her transition into condo living.

Every organizational project starts with the idea that there needs to be a change. That idea can spring from necessity or just a willingness to want more from your life and space, but the journey can be long, and it isn't always easy. What motivates you to move forward? It could be a move, like Queen Hodgepodge, or maybe you are merging two households. You might be an empty nester. In all of these situations, you have major decisions to make about your house, office, or car.

Maybe you are motivated because of time management. Your life feels stressful because you have too much "stuff" clogging your space, cluttering your mind, and taking too much time out of your life. You feel crazy opening a drawer or a closet because you can't easily locate anything you need. Maybe you are on a perpetual search for some random item that you misplaced and, because nothing you own has a system, finding it is next to impossible in any reasonable timeframe. You could be motivated to release and let go, because none of these items are adding value to your existence. Instead, they are taking away your energy and calm.

So, what can you do to keep yourself motivated? One way is to visualize what you want for your new space. Creating a vision board—also known as a dream board, vision map, or treasure map—can aid you in this, as it is a visual manifestation of your dreams and goals. It is a collage of images or pictures that inspire you to conceptualize your goals and create your dreams. This is also a great way to generate new energy if you're feeling a little blocked in the creative process. Be sure to put as many details as possible on your vision board. The more details, the better.

Your vision board can also help you focus and offer you a sense of direction about your future. What would your vision of your home be if you had no clutter and things were organized? How does this vision make you feel? Free, clear, and inspired? Peaceful and positive? By creating a vision for your new life, you are expressing yourself, which will help you feel prepared and confident about the future.

The great news is that you are motivated and ready to make a change. So, put on some music, set your timer for three hours, and see what you can accomplish!

Go for it! Why NOT you? Change your space, change your life. Get in that closet and start purging stuff that no longer serves you. It is exciting to be in control of where you are going. You have choices to make to move forward, so make those choices and change yourself.

See how you feel after cleaning, purging, and organizing. It's like you are a new being. Yes, this process *is* cathartic.

Chapter 8

It's a Closet Affair

"Your Majesty, the castle has been cleaned and organized, just as you decreed, and with a full week to spare!" Queen Hodgepodge proudly declared while standing before the king. The castle was now ready for them to move! She was as excited as she was nervous, and she couldn't wait to hear King Haywire give her the praise she craved for having completed this monumental task.

The king, with anticipation on his face, said, "Walk me around the castle and show me what you've done!"

She led him through the castle. Dungeon to bedrooms, all was clean, well lit, and organized. Queen Hodgepodge simply beamed with pride!

He didn't say anything until they were at the end of the "tour" in their bedroom. "Very nicely done, dear!" The king actually looked happy. "I do have one question, though."

"Certainly, dear. Anything," she said. She now felt a sense of impending doom. Had she missed something? Or worse, had she gotten rid of something of his that he now wanted?

He stepped over to her closet door and reached for it. She knew right then what she had left out. "Didn't you forget something?" he asked, slowly opening the door.

The queen's closet was, by far, the worst room in the house. She was a clothes hoarder. She owned so many gowns and shoes that she truthfully didn't know what all she had. And jewelry! My goodness, she had jewelry. How was she ever going to go through it all?

"Yes," she answered, "it appears that I have. I will get right on it and get it clean."

"I can see what you have done so far, and I am impressed with you and the hard work you have put into it." The king went on, "But, as you stated yourself, you only have a week to get this done. And from the looks of it, you may need every second of it."

She was both relieved and mortified by that statement. *A week may not be enough time!* This was a BIG closet, and she had no idea how to get started. She didn't want any help on this room, as it was her most personal.

She sat down to cry, but then realized that this was just another large task that needed to be broken down and conquered.

***

While there is no quick fix for clearing out a closet (all the clothes must eventually be gone through), Queen Hodgepodge did receive advice for what to keep and how to use her personal style to streamline her clothing choices. She began to work on her closet by putting a system in place. She designated three large, plastic bags just for clothes: one bag to give away, another bag for trash, and one bag to give to her best friend Princess Paisley.

First, get rid of clothes that do not fit. Then, eliminate the clothes that are dated. Once these tasks are done, you need to choose outfits with the greatest flexibility, items that can be worn with others to create more than a single look or outfit. Eliminate certain articles of clothing if:

- They do not fit properly or do not flatter your body.
- They need mending or have stains.
- You've never felt like a queen in this piece of clothing.

You must be honest with yourself when it comes to clothes you cannot currently wear. Ask yourself the following questions:

- *Will I ever really take the time and money to get the item repaired?*
- *Will I ever lose enough weight to fit into it?*

Being realistic helps with this process. **If you haven't worn an item in two years, then you probably won't ever again, and it's time to get rid of it!** Give any discarded clothing to a thrift store, or donate them to people in need. Have a permanent bag in your closet for items you no longer wear.

Starting this process at the turn of the season will help, as you can deal with cool/warm-weather clothes one season at a time. This will also make deciding what to give away easier, as you can give yourself until the end of the season to decide if you want to keep something. This will minimize the amount of clothes storage you have to manage.

A well-organized closet is a gift to yourself, and categorizing is key. First, group like items together: shirts, pants, skirts, dresses, etc. Then, separate them by season: e.g. short, quarter, and long sleeve. Next, have all the clothes facing the same way, as it is easier and faster to see what you have if they are all facing in the same direction. Finally, put all items on hangers of the same shape and size, as it will make them much easier to look through when coordinating outfits. By implementing a system for the daily use of your closet, you will save both time and stress when getting ready in the morning. That will allow you to start your day in a more positive state of mind.

It's not only our clothes that can get junked up in a closet; jewelry often finds its way into the nooks and crannies of our dressers and drawers. Go through your jewelry and dispose of broken costume jewelry. Make plans to sell any jewelry you don't wear. For fine jewelry, consider having it appraised, as it may be of value.

The system that Queen Hodgepodge came up with:

- Sort the clothes by type (shirts, pants, dresses, etc.).
- Sort clothes based on the two-year rule.
- Give away usable items you are not keeping.
- Sort what is left by seasons.
- Store items not in season by hanging or folding them properly and placing them in an appropriate storage spot.

Queen Hodgepodge's maintenance plan:

- When the items get dirty, put them into the laundry hamper.
- Do the laundry that has accumulated on a regular basis.
- Wash, dry, fold, and put the now-clean items away. (This is the hard part of the system, as it requires time.)
- If applicable, pick a day or two during the month to address any dry cleaning. (This will help keep all your clothes clean and ready for your next big event!)

Tips for Creating a Closet System

- Keep a "donate bag" in your closet in which to place clothes you just do not want in your life anymore. The clothes could be too small, not in style, need repair, etc. Get it out of YOUR closet, since you want your closet looking royal like the rest of your house!
- Have a laundry basket in your closet, so when you change you can put dirty clothes immediately into a sorted system.
- After you declutter your closet, decide if you need any containers for storing items. I prefer clear containers that you can see the contents inside of and on which you can change the labels.
- A nice addition to a closet is lavender sachets. They keep the moths away, and your closet will smell fresh and clean.

AFFIRMATIONS AND EXERCISES FOR GROWTH

MIND: Think of how to get the most use out of every piece of clothing. How many ways can you wear a specific blouse or shirt? Classics like blue jeans never go out of style and can easily be "spruced up" by adding a fashionable shirt, jacket, or belt.

BODY: Keep the two-year rule in play. Set up a specific time of year to go through your clothes, such as during seasonal changes. Consider hiring an organizer to help with this, as it can quickly become an overwhelming project.

SPIRIT: Don't put your energy into the negative feelings that may arise from releasing certain items from your wardrobe. Instead, focus on the positive effects of releasing these items that no longer serve your spirit.

CHAPTER 8 ACTION PLAN

- List your strengths and weaknesses when it comes to cleaning closets.

Strengths	Weaknesses

- Use this flow chart when going through your clothing items to determine what will be done with them:

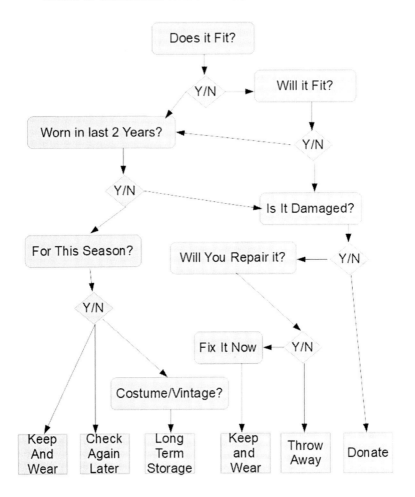

- Separate your jewelry into sections, such as fine jewelry and costume jewelry, and decide what to keep, get rid of, or give to family.
- What is your system for organizing jewelry?
_____
_____

Chapter 9

Kitchen Catch-all

"HODGEPODGE!" King Haywire bellowed louder than his queen had ever heard. He wasn't happy, a fact she could pick up on all the way in the library.

Queen Hodgepodge practically sprinted into the kitchen to see what had the king so upset. Out of breath and panting, she stammered, "Y-yes?"

The king, face red with anger, said, "Where is my university stein? I want some beer, and I want to drink it out of my favorite stein! Where is it?"

"You told me to get rid of all of the clutter and, *since you haven't used that old stein in over a year*, I thought you would be okay without it," said the queen. "Besides, the handle was cracked, and it would have broken as soon as you filled it up and drank from it. So, I actually *saved* you from embarrassment in front of the court. You should be thanking me." The queen felt more emboldened than she had ever dared to be. After all, this was ridiculous, and she wasn't going to let him have things both ways: clean the house of all clutter, but just not of *his* things.

King Haywire, caught off-guard, didn't really know how to handle this development, so he just said, "Harrumph! Very well, but I still need something to hold my beer!"

"Then use one of the other fifty steins that we still have. They are all perfectly good at holding beer!" With that, she turned and walked out of the room.

***

Even in a castle, the kitchen is the heart and soul of the home. It is arguably the most important room in the house. The kitchen also seems to be the place where everything ends up (hence the "junk drawer" present in every house). What is your system for kitchen clutter? Do you have a dragon keeping you from making a system? Do not be afraid to establish a system or hire an organizing sorcerer to help you get rid of the fiery dragons that are huffing and puffing at you to not be successful.

The number-one challenge seen in kitchens is counter clutter. Do you currently have a system for maintaining your countertops? Perhaps your method is to clear all items on the counters before you eat. Maybe you clean the counters after you finish the dishes, or maybe you address them in the morning. If you let it hang around until the morning, then that is what you wake up to. Not the best way to start your day.

Figuring out what is and is not working can be daunting, but if there is a mess, you just need a process! It can be a simple one, but you need to develop a system to regain your countertops and transform the rest of your kitchen into a clear, uncluttered space.

Be sure that anything you are not using daily does not end up on your counter. If needed, keep nonessential items in a drawer to help keep your counters clear and your appliances accessible. It is also important to periodically clear out your kitchen cupboards. Reorganizing and letting go of things you are not using in the kitchen cupboards will eliminate clutter and the need for more shelving. You can easily do it on your own. Start by just taking it one shelf at a time. Remember your "piles" and decide to keep, toss, or give away. The most important part of organizing a kitchen is to categorize your items. Keep like items with like items! Cups, plates, glasses, and silverware should all be kept in a place close to the dishwasher for better time management and efficiency.

One of the best organizational tips in the kitchen is to have NO dirty dishes in the sink. Clean dishes immediately after use—either by washing with soap or placing directly into the dishwasher—to keep your sink clear of dirty dishes at all times. After running the dishwasher, unload it immediately so that it is clear to use. Simply keeping the dishes washed and cleared can save time and help keep your kitchen from becoming too cluttered. It also helps to keep you from becoming too overwhelmed and tired to maintain these chores.

While a refrigerator may be one of the most essential appliances in your kitchen, it can also be one of the messier tasks to take on. What does your refrigerator look like right now? Clean and clear? Or, is it a place where bad recipes go to die? Perhaps it is a breeding ground for science experiments, replete with unrecognizable food products that have turned to slime in leftover containers! Be truthful with yourself.

No matter the state your refrigerator is in, it *can* be cleaned and organized. All it takes is a little effort to transform your fridge into a clean, healthy space that everyone can use easily. It only takes a once-a-week check. One day each week, check the dates on food, leftovers, and takeout. Check your fruit and vegetable bins, too, and toss items that are expired or no longer fresh. That's all there is to it! Now you can go shopping and refill with fresh items that you know you need.

One helpful idea is to place all food items in see-through storage containers so that you can see what is in them. Be sure that you are labeling and dating items, as well, so that you know what is fresh and what needs to go. Keep labels and pens near the refrigerator so you can easily label new items.

Categorizing your food items is also very important. Once you do this, you will have a blueprint of where your food needs to be placed. Drinks need a shelf, fruits and veggies need a bin, and then have a drawer for meats and dairy. Leftovers and condiments can go on shelves or in door bins as needed. Now it is easy to see what is in your refrigerator! That comes in handy when planning meals and going grocery shopping.

Baking soda helps get rid of odors in the refrigerator and sink drains. Just pour it down the drain so it smells fresh and clean!

As for refrigerator art, everyone has some—some more than others. There are known instances of so much artwork on the refrigerator that it looks like a scrapbook work center. The artwork doesn't need to go, but it does need to be minimized. Have a section of the door for the artwork to be proudly displayed, and only keep up the most recent pieces.

The rule is: If your refrigerator is too cluttered on the outside, be very afraid of the inside. It can be like a minefield of stuff, and something may explode on you.

The two main items to keep *on* the refrigerator are recipes and a whiteboard that all the family members can write on for a food list. If it's not on the list, don't buy it. You can even take a picture of the food list each week. That way, you don't even have to write anything down when you go to the store. This is an easy way to keep track of the family's grocery needs, as well.

The system that Queen Hodgepodge came up with:

- Wash all dishes at the end of each meal.
- Dry clean dishes and put them away.
- Throw away unwanted items.
- Store items that aren't used every day.

Queen Hodgepodge's maintenance plan:

- When kitchen items get dirty, put them into the soapy water bowl.
- After each meal, do the dishes that have accumulated.

- Wash, dry, and put the clean dishes away. (This is the hard part of the system, as it requires time.)
- Wipe down all counters and put small appliances back in their designated spots.

AFFIRMATIONS AND EXERCISES FOR GROWTH

MIND: Find ways to make the most of each appliance so that you need less of them. The less scattered your space, the less scattered your mind.

BODY: Now that you have a clean, uncluttered kitchen, relax and enjoy the space. Take this new opportunity to have people over or plan an event.

SPIRIT: Use your new space to try out a new recipe, as cooking can be calming and very soulful.

CHAPTER 9 ACTION PLAN

- Make a checklist for weekly/daily kitchen chores, such as:
    - Trash (weekly)
    - Dishwasher (once or twice a week, depending on household)
    - Check leftovers (weekly)
    - Throw out expired food (weekly)
    - Wipe down sink (weekly)
    - Wipe down fridge (weekly)
    - Clear/wipe down counters (daily)
    - Clean food-prep devices such as coffee pots, toasters, etc. (daily)
    - Clean microwave oven (weekly)
    - Sweep/mop floor (weekly)

- Once a month, clear expired announcements, invitations, coupons, etc. off the fridge.
- Set an intention to address kitchen chores in the evening after dinner. Prep lunches for the next day while preparing dinner to save yourself time and cleanup. This will make your mornings less stressful and more efficient.

Chapter 10

Clearing the Carriage

Before King Haywire had a chance to see his royal carriage, Queen Hodgepodge made her way to the garage to make absolutely certain that it was clean and organized. They had servants to do this, but the queen didn't want to take ANY chances.

"Is the royal carriage clean?" she asked the royal carriage keeper.

"Why, yes it is, Your Majesty."

"Does it have all of the necessary items, like wine, glasses, the money box, napkins, and an icebox for the king's snacks? Are the drapes cleaned and properly draped?"

Sighing under his breath, the keeper answered, "Yes, Your Majesty. I keep a list of everything that needs to be done to the carriage—both before the king needs it and after. I also make sure that it is operating properly, as I do not want it to break down with you or the king inside."

"Very well. Show me, please."

***

Everyone needs a way to get around. Queen Hodgepodge drives a carriage coupe, but you might have a truck, sedan, boat, or plane! Is it hard to find the ignition because of the garbage piled up between your seats? Is your car a dumpster on wheels? Does it cause you stress if anyone asks for a ride? Maybe you're too embarrassed to even let anyone in it.

Like the good friend your car is, it deserves respect. Keeping your car clean and organized will help you enjoy driving again. When you get your car washed, vacuumed, and organized, you feel like you have a new car! Wouldn't it be great to have this feeling every time you get in your car? Just like your house, your car needs to be organized.

Keep a bag for trash nearby so you can dispose of things when necessary; it'll be a huge help. Also, keep a small plastic tub in the vehicle to fill with all the miscellaneous stuff that tends to pile up, like pens, receipts, parking stubs, etc. Then at the end of every day, bring it inside and empty it. Return it to the car for the next day, because having loose items in your car is distracting. It would also be beneficial to keep a second container for items that need to stay in the car all the time.

Items to keep inside the cabin include (but are not limited to) hand sanitizer, a flashlight, nonperishable food items like raisins or nuts, water, and change for troll tolls. Things to keep in a container in the trunk might include glass cleaner, paper towels, a first-aid kit, and a lightweight blanket.

If you are the kind of person who finds themselves in the car quite often, it might also help to have a change of clothes and a comfortable pair of shoes in a bag of some type, just in case. Even Queen Hodgepodge keeps a trunk full of essentials in her carriage.

When things are clean, it makes you feel refreshed, and having an organization system for your vehicle ensures that every time you get in, you feel good because it is clear, clean, and ready to go.

The system that Queen Hodgepodge came up with:

- Have a medium-sized bag available for trash.

- Make a list of needed items for the cabin and the trunk.
  - Laminate the list and leave it in the glovebox to ensure that everything has been accounted for.
  - Good items to have as a "just in case" backup are a good blanket, hat, gloves, extra clothes, and a jacket.
- Do not leave any opened food in the carriage overnight.
- Make sure all tools in the trunk are operating properly.
  - At minimum you need a flathead and Philips screwdriver, small wrench and socket set, jumper cables, flashlight (with extra batteries), a roll of duct tape, a roll of electrical tape, and a hammer.

Queen Hodgepodge's maintenance plan:

- When the items get used, replace them.
- Check tools for rust and proper functioning on a regular basis.
  - A small toolbox is needed to hold the tools and ensure that they are where they need to be.

AFFIRMATIONS AND EXERCISES FOR GROWTH

MIND: Having a good set of tools and emergency supplies in your car allows you to travel worry-free.

BODY: Keeping your car clean makes it easier for you to relax and concentrate on driving.

SPIRIT: When your car is clean and full of the proper supplies, you are free to travel to wherever the spirit takes you.

CHAPTER 10 ACTION PLAN

- Pick a day of the week to address your car: _____
- Set reminders for servicing the wipers, tires, oil, etc.
- Pick two days out of the month to wash/vacuum your car; e.g. the first and fifteenth: _____
- Organize your car with the following items:
    - Trash receptacle
    - Bin containing the following:
        - _____
        - _____
        - _____

Chapter 11

Freedom in Your Workplace

Enjoying the day, Queen Hodgepodge rode through the downtown area of the kingdom in the royal carriage. As she looked out the window, they happened to pass the regal office building. The queen was thinking about the office when suddenly she bolted upright and screamed for the driver to pull over. She had completely forgotten the office in all the madness trying to get the castle cleaned and organized! What was she going to do? The king was planning to come down to the office in a couple of days, and she just *couldn't* let him see the mess it was currently in.

"Take me to the office!" she demanded of the driver.

"Yes, Your Highness. At once!"

They turned around and went back to the office, where the queen was almost afraid to go in. How could she possibly get it cleaned and organized in a couple of days? The old dragons began to creep up on her, and she started to panic.

She walked into the office to see what her fear told her was an insurmountable task. Yet to her surprise, as she started to look around she found herself already organizing the clutter and mess into "throw away," "keep," and "store" piles in her mind. All the work with the McOrganizing Sorceress had paid off! Hodgepodge now knew that she could deal with this; she knew that clutter and mess would never again rule her life.

She started in the lobby and worked her way back, going room by room until she was done. Wow! That wasn't even hard! Queen Hodgepodge was relieved that the lessons the McOrganizing Sorceress had taught her were now just a part of her life. She was no longer bound by those ugly dragons.

***

Queen Hodgepodge had kept hidden yet another great challenge in her life: office clutter. Along with piles and piles of paperwork and bills, she had saved pictures of clothing, party ideas, new makeup, etc. everywhere! She began her project by setting up a workspace with all her necessary sorting materials.

As with anything, you will still need a system for decluttering your space and reorganizing it after. First, gather your boxes or bags for sorting and eliminating unneeded items. Label them with categories like "file," "long-term storage," "short-term storage," "recycle or shred"—whichever configuration best suits your needs.

Second, pick an area you want to focus on. The queen decided to start with her oversized bookshelf because for her, paperwork is daunting, and she was confused about what needed to be eliminated or stored long term. While sorting, she placed the items according to the labeled boxes, which really helped her feel more in control of her mess and her space. She completed organizing her bookshelf in three hours!

Because everyone's office space is unique to them and the type of work they do, this chapter will be broken into subtopics of things that one might find in their office. We will then discuss how to address each item accordingly.

ORGANIZING MAIL

What should be done about mail? Everyone gets it. Queen Hodgepodge loves getting mail from faraway lands. She personally loves hearing from Castleco, her favorite discount warehouse store, and *Crowns and Tiaras Monthly*. However, mail is full of potential clutter just ready to overtake your counters and tables. It presents a challenge not just for Queen Hodgepodge, but for many people. Anyone who receives mail—whether "snail mail," package delivery, or emails—must have a system and use it daily. Remember, you are not broken, but your mail-retrieval system might be. If you have a system that works, it should take no longer than five minutes per day to deal with the mail.

The key is to deal with the mail as soon as you retrieve it. The most important concept in formulating a system for your mail is to have one spot where all mail-related items go. Pick a convenient and accessible place and keep a shredder (or a gremlin with sharp teeth) in the same area to get rid of items containing personal information and account numbers. Have your calendar on hand to enter invites and event dates that you receive in the mail. For sorting your mail, purchase three different color bins, and make sure they are an appropriate size and can easily be distinguished and labeled. Organize the three bins accordingly:

- First bin: discard magazines (this type of paper needs to be separate at the recycling center, so it gets its own bin).
- Second bin: discard "regular mail."
- Third bin: as an inbox for bills that need to be paid, correspondence, and items to file. This could be labeled as your "take action" bin.

It is very important that you delve into your "take action" box on the first and the fifteenth of the month. Now would also be the time to pay the bills. Bill collectors don't care how much clutter you have; they only care if you're paying your bills! Get your checkbook out, pay the bills, and file your records away in your "paid" file. Switching your bills to automatic bill pay is also a great way to speed up this process. If you enjoy catalogs and magazines, you can skip the bins and place them wherever you like to read them: a nightstand by the bed, the bathroom, a magazine rack, etc. When the reading materials become overwhelming in number, purge them and replace with the new. Remember to discard any unwanted items, such as junk mail, in the first and second bins, then place anything requiring a response in the "take action" bin.

Now, onto the high tech!

Emails are still a form of mail, and as such need to be read and dealt with every work day. As far as emails, or anything web-related is concerned, remember: "If you don't need it, delete it!" Again, keep your calendar close at hand to enter the dates of meetings and activities. It is easier and quicker to declutter your email if you sort it first. Luckily, sorting emails is as simple as the click of your mouse, and doing so will allow you to quickly delete a bunch of unrelated and unwanted emails at once.

One way to eliminate email overload is to unsubscribe from mailing lists that are no longer relevant or interesting, or to ones you no longer have the time to read regularly. Only let your inbox contain emails that you truly enjoy, you have time to read, or that are relevant to your current life situation. Save checking emails for the morning and once again in the afternoon. Feeling forced to check it every hour will interrupt your work flow. Be sure to stay away from social media while dealing with email, as it can be distracting and take you down a rabbit hole. Make these changes, and you'll be delighted with how much time you save! By spending just a little time addressing the mail, you can keep your papers sorted so that your sanity isn't *distorted*!

It is important to remember that while a system is important for dealing with the lack of physical organization, there is also usually a lack of mental or spiritual organization, as well. For example, at Prince Random's home office, he had collected stacks of mail up to five years old, despite the fact that the rest of his home was clean and tidy. It turns out that his wife had divorced him around the same time he started hoarding the mail. As he recalled the chronology, the revelation helped him to work through his attachment and let go of the mail. The processing and getting rid of it helped him with his delayed grieving process. He felt that the results gave him clarity on both a physical and emotional level.

Every step you take to declutter your life will advance you physically, mentally, and spiritually. Breathe deep and affirm that clearing mail from your life will open up your life to new possibilities and probabilities.

ORGANIZING GENERAL PAPERWORK

Paperwork is one of the most challenging parts to any office organization project. Everybody has it, and it can be very anxiety inducing. What to keep and for how long, what to shred, what's important to find at a moment's notice, and how to store it all in the meantime are just a few common questions that come up in the process. As a general rule, the following will be considered important documents that you should know the location of and have access to:

- Tax documents (keep at least seven years)
- Castle deeds
- Carriage bill of sale
- Birth certificates
- Passports
- Receipts from major purchases
- Documents related to any major remodeling projects

One really efficient way to manage all of your paper clutter is to scan it into your computer. This is especially true of important documents, so that you can organize them on your computer and obtain a copy whenever you need.

ORGANIZING BOOKS

Go through your bookshelf and gather any books you haven't touched in months, or any books that you have no intention of ever rereading. Be realistic and completely ruthless. If you haven't touched it in a year, you're most likely not going to read it again. Sell the books on Amazon, Craigslist, or eBay. You can even trade them online with other book lovers or donate them to your local library or charity.

ORGANIZING NOTEBOOKS

Offices usually have a ton of notebooks lying around. Look at them and throw out the ones that you no longer want or need. Most notebooks are filled with notes from classes or meetings attended. Shred everything confidential and recycle the rest. Or, if the notebooks are new or barely used, maybe you know a school teacher that could benefit from them.

ORGANIZING OLD OR UNUSED ELECTRONICS

Invariably, every office has a drawer full of old cords and boxes of old keyboards and computer parts that are no longer relevant or needed. Almost any computer store will be happy to help recycle these parts, so that is the best place for them, not some dumpster.

ORGANIZING OLD OFFICE FURNITURE

As time goes by, furniture can get worn and make the office space look old and out of date. Furniture needs to be donated to Goodwill or some other charity where it can be reused. Another way to take care of old, outdated furniture is to resurface it. Slipcovers on couches and chairs can not only brighten up the office with clean looks, but they can also add some much-needed color to a drab place.

***

The system that Queen Hodgepodge came up with:

- Go through all the magazines, notebooks, and piles of paper to sort them into appropriate piles.
- Clean out all drawers and get rid of anything not needed.
- Throw away unusable items.
- Give away usable items you are not keeping.
- Change out, repair, or rearrange old furniture as needed.

Queen Hodgepodge's maintenance plan:

- Go through the papers and magazines once a month and get rid of anything you don't need (file or shred if need be).
- Check the furniture for any necessary repairs on a regular basis.

AFFIRMATIONS AND EXERCISES FOR GROWTH

MIND: Clearing your office clutter will help you to be more productive when you're working. This will lead to an increase in office productivity and motivation at work.

BODY: You will be able to relax more in a clean office space.

SPIRIT: When work can be done quickly and without stress, it allows you to truly take time off for yourself without any lingering anxiety.

CHAPTER 11 ACTION PLAN

- Buy and label three bins for sorting mail. Use these bins for your magazine mail, regular mail, and your "take action" bin.
- Unsubscribe from any unnecessary emailing lists once a month.
- On the first and fifteenth of the month, address bills and get them paid (or, if online, schedule them to be paid).

Chapter 12

The Nuts and Bolts of Organizing

Matilda, a friend of the queen, invited her to a dinner party last week. While Queen Hodgepodge was at Matilda's house, she noticed that dishes were piled up on every surface in the kitchen. Wasn't she planning an eight-course meal for the party? This made the queen very anxious for Matilda, because there seemed to be no method to the madness in all the clutter.

Using the information that she had learned from the McOrganizing Sorceress, the queen went to work helping her friend. First, they needed to make sure the dishes were all cleaned and sorted by like items. Next, they found a place to store unneeded dishes that would be easily accessible and maintained. Now the dishes they were going to need were ready for the evening. Because some of the plates may be used more than once, a system was required for cleaning them, as well.

Matilda was amazed that Queen Hodgepodge was able to come up with a plan and accomplish it so quickly.

"It's all in a days' work for a queen!" Hodgepodge said. "It is looking the dragons in the eyes and not backing down. Look at it as a game with a bunch of small parts, not as a single task that is overwhelming. Now, let's get these dishes into the cabinets in an orderly fashion so that we can use them tonight!"

***

It is so important to have established systems employed throughout the home or office. If no systems are in place for regular life activities, you may become nervous, frustrated, and angry. Ask yourself where your toothbrush is; do you know the exact location? Where do you keep your silverware? How about your car keys? These seem like items you would obviously remember, so if you know exactly where your toothbrush, silverware, and keys are, why not make a system for your office, mail, grocery shopping, laundry, trash, car maintenance, etc.?

To make a system, you need to identify *where* you need a system. Regarding organizing, a system is a method to help you tackle daily activities and sort your belongings in such a way that they can be easily accessed and used. A characteristic of a good system is that anyone can come into the space and use the system themselves. In this instance, Matilda needed to develop a system for her dishes. If she were to design a system that allows her to clean the dishes and put them away on a regular basis, this would make it possible to find the dishes when they are needed. This system would add efficiency to her life, cutting down on stress and frustration.

A system is a tool that adds clarity to your space and your daily comings and goings. Systems tackle disorder and chaos in your life, leaving you free to spend your time and energy on other endeavors. However, a system is not going to remain in place without some upkeep and regular attention.

When you have a system, it is important that everyone involved with utilizing the space helps to maintain that system. Communication is very important. It is important that everyone understands how the system works and how to keep up with it. It is also important for the system to be designed to meet everyone's needs. When it does not, or those needs change, the system can cease to be effective. At this point, the system needs to be reviewed, changed to meet the new requirements, or scrapped.

If your systems are no longer working for you or you're having a hard time developing strong systems for your space, it might be beneficial to hire an organizer to help you. They can take something that is messy, chaotic, and unordered, and rearrange it logically into a structured, coherent system so that it meets the requirements of the space.

Let's use Matilda and her dish problem as an example. Dishes were all over the counters; some were clean while others were not. How could anyone know if a dish could be used like that?

The system that Queen Hodgepodge helped Matilda come up with:

- Wash all the dishes and sort them into like stacks. (Each type of dish now has a place with all other dishes like it.)
- Wipe down all the cabinets that the dishes can go in, and lay down a nonslip mat in each. (The mat helps the dishes to not slide around when the top dish is pulled out to use.)
- Decide where each type of dish needs to go based on ease of access and frequency of use. (The most used dishes get the easiest place to access.)
- Place the dishes into the cabinets in neat, organized stacks that are not too high. (The top dish needs to be able to come off the top without removing the entire pile.)

Queen Hodgepodge's maintenance plan:

- Once a dish (or dishes) has been used, it needs to be placed in the sink or dishwasher to be washed. (This allows others to see that the dish is dirty without having to pick it up.)
- Once or twice a day (as needed), the dishes are to be

washed, dried, and put away. (This is the hard part of the system, as it requires taking the time to do it.)

CREATING ORGANIZING SYSTEMS TIPS

- Look at the task that needs a system.
    - What is the desired outcome?
    - What is the *last* step to getting that desired outcome?
    - What is the step *right before the last one*? (Continue asking this question until you are at the beginning.)
- Employ the KISS method (Keep It Super Simple).
    - Can the steps you just came up with be reduced in *any* way that will not affect the outcome? (Remove any unneeded steps.)
    - The simpler the system, the easier it is to install (and maintain).
    - Ask someone else for help.
- Put the plan in place and test it out.
    - Does it work like you thought? (Adjust as needed.)
    - Once your system is in place and working, write it down in a notebook. (This will be a reminder for you, if you need it.)
- If you are having problems coming up with a plan, consult the notebook. (Use it as a guide for creating future systems.)

GRAB 'N' GO BAG

Now that everything has a place and a routine, it's a good time to address what to do when confronted with chaos. Everyone in your family needs a "grab 'n' go" bag. Having this bag gives you quick access to clothing, blankets, food rations, and a medical kit, and it prepares you for a disaster in which evacuation is necessary.

Both parents and children should keep their individual bags in their own rooms, and it is recommended that twice a year the bags be gone through to make sure they are kept current. You will need to keep photocopies of the following in waterproof containers:

- Driver's license
- House deed
- Birth certificates
- Marriage certificate
- Proof of insurance
- Medical records
- Passports
- SS cards
- List of personal contacts
- Maps of the area

It will also be important to have copies of house keys and car keys, an envelope full of cash, credit cards, important family photos, family jewelry, a camera, a radio, headlamps or flashlights (with batteries), matches or a lighter (kept waterproof), pens and paper, toiletries, medicines, vitamins, some nonperishable food items, and maybe even a pack of playing cards.

Be sure that any pets are all microchipped and have ID information on their collars and in their own grab 'n' go bags: leashes, medications, meal bowls, and three days' worth of food and water.

AFFIRMATIONS AND EXERCISES FOR GROWTH

MIND: Not everything needs a written system in place. Don't overthink this and become trapped by systems. Use systems for things you are having issues with, such as laundry, dishes, mail, etc.

BODY: Walk through each system you come up with to assess its practicality. Only keep systems you need.

SPIRIT: Keep repeating to yourself that this process is going easily and effortlessly, with peace and harmony. As you get used to the systems you choose to have in place, you will feel more in control of your life.

CHAPTER 12 ACTION PLAN

- Identify any existing systems you may have and whether or not they are working.
  _____
  _____
  _____
  _____
  _____

- Make a list of zones that still need systems.
  1. _____
  2. _____
  3. _____
  4. _____
  5. _____

- Be sure to communicate your systems to everyone who will be using them. If the systems are not maintained, they will fall apart

Chapter 13

Organizing with Children

Now that Queen Hodgepodge and King Haywire were all moved out of the castle, it was time for their daughter Princess Persnickety to take over the kingdom and move into the castle with her husband and their two children. Because it is never too early to teach your children good household habits, Hodgepodge took it upon herself to teach her grandkids all of her new skills so that the castle would stay as pristine as the queen had left it.

The following are ways that you, too, can assist your kids in keeping your house organized and functional for everyone.

- Keep a family calendar and have the child refer to the calendar when making plans. Your child can have his or her own planner/calendar, as this will be good for learning time management.
- Daily routines instill discipline. The more the child gets familiarized with routine, the more success you both will have.
- Having your child perform daily chores, like loading the dishwasher and caring for and feeding pets, helps prepare him or her for their future as a roommate, spouse, or per-

haps your elder care provider! This is teaching them a lifelong skill set that everyone will be thankful for when they're older.

- Having a homework routine will make accomplishing this task easier. Set up a desk and workspace where they can do schoolwork daily at the same place and time in a comfortable environment. If your child does not have homework, you can use this time for reading, puzzle solving, or learning a foreign language.
- Teach your child to organize their items the night before an activity.
    - Lay clothing out.
    - Have all items necessary for that day in one location.
    - Pack backpack for school and afterschool activities.
    - Prep lunch and snacks.

- Have them check their backpack daily to see what lurks in there. This teaches your child to pay attention to their items and keep up with their personal tasks. Things labeled with colors help your child locate things more quickly.
- Guide your child through their closet and drawers, and teach them how to organize.
- Teach your child how not to attack the whole project, instead breaking it down into smaller increments. This will help to reduce anxiety for the both of you. Divide and conquer! Making to-do lists is helpful for focusing on what you need to do.
- The benefits to teaching your child organization skills:
    - Experience less overall stress
    - Perform better academically
    - Better time management

- Sharper focus
- Less frustration

Through roleplaying, teach your child how good organization makes them shine and sparkle amongst their peers!

AFFIRMATIONS AND EXERCISES FOR GROWTH

MIND: You will find more harmony in your relationships with your children by instilling in them beneficial life skills and routines at an early age.

BODY: There will be less stress on your physical space when your family is working as a team to maintain it and keep it clutter-free.

SPIRIT: When there is familial harmony, you can achieve a greater sense of personal harmony, as you will now have more time to focus within.

CHAPTER 13 ACTION PLAN

- Allocate some time to sit down with your children and explain to them what a calendar is, and how your family's calendar works. Make it fun for them by employing the use of stickers and bright colors to plan appointments and set reminders for events.
- Create a chore wheel with your kids that tells them what their responsibilities will be for that week. You can make it fun by turning it into a game and setting up a rewards system.
- Spend one night a week making a kid-friendly recipe with your children for dinner. This will not only be good family time together, but it will help to encourage healthy eating habits and self-sufficiency.

Conclusion

Queen Hodgepodge's journey is one that we can all learn something from. She faced the dastardly Dragons of Contention by making choices that freed her from the paralysis of moving forward and completing organizational tasks. She knew she did not initially have the skill set required to make an organizational blueprint for downsizing to a condo, but after contacting the McOrganizing Sorceress, Hodgepodge had the catalyst she needed to deal with her clogged-up energy and frustrated routines. Learning new ways of dealing with attachment to items and resistance to the organizing process helped her move forward with her goals. Releasing the cobwebs in her mind helped her to both physically and spiritually clear clutter in her life.

As Queen Hodgepodge clearly shows, there are no hopeless organizational cases. Everyone can change their space. Yes, everyone! By learning some basic organizational skills, you, too, can conquer your dragons and face your fears in your own journey to clarity. The inspiration that I want you to take from this book is that you are the queen or king of your castle, and you can control your clutter so your clutter doesn't control you.

The End

About the Author

Growing up, McPatti noticed her affinity for organizing and maintaining order. People would often comment on how organized she was! However, she never realized just how apparent these talents were until about ten years ago, when a guest to her home called and asked who organized and staged the house. After revealing she had done all the work herself, the person invited McPatti to her house to help organize it. It was then that she realized she could use this special set of skills to help others organize their lives, too, and boy would she have job security!

McPatti lives in Atlanta, Georgia, with her husband, son, and fabulous black cat Miss Meowster. Today, when not organizing and staging or writing and lecturing, she teaches yoga and sings in various choirs.